D0582113

ELECTRIC TRAINS

A POCKET HISTORY

ROBIN JONES

Dedicated to Vicky and Ross

First published in Great Britain in 2010

Copyright © 2010 Diamond Head Productions

British Library Cataloguing-in-Publication Data
A CIP record for this title is available from the British Library

ISBN 978 1 906887 81 0

PiXZ Books
Halsgrove House, Ryelands Industrial Estate,
Bagley Road, Wellington, Somerset TA21 9PZ
Tel: 01823 653777
Fax: 01823 216796
email: sales@halsgrove.com

An imprint of Halstar Ltd, part of the Halsgrove group of companies
Information on all Halsgrove titles is available at: www.halsgrove.com

Printed and bound in China by Toppan Leefung Printing Ltd

Introduction

Everyone knows that Britain invented the steam locomotive. The best-known of all early locomotives, George Stephenson's *Rocket* of 1829, while being a watershed in transport technology, was not the first. It was in 1804 that Cornish mining engineer Richard Trevithick gave his first public demonstration of a steam locomotive, on the Penydarren Tramroad near Merthyr Tydfil. Steam traction revolutionised railways, which hitherto had been little local horse-drawn affairs often linking mines and factories to canals, ports and harbours.

Yet while Britain was gripped by the great period of railway building of the 1830s and '40s in which many of our inter-city routes began to take shape, there were those who believed that the future lay beyond steam haulage. In 1835, blacksmith Thomas Davenport of Vermont, USA, exhibited a small railway operated by a miniature electric motor. Two years later, Scotsman Robert Davidson built a model electric locomotive, and followed it up with a four-wheeled machine, *Galavani*, that was powered by zinc-acid batteries. It was tested on the Edinburgh-Glasgow line in September 1842 and reached 4mph – but it was found that its consumption of zinc was 40 times more expensive than burning coal in a steam engine. It was, nevertheless, the world's first electric locomotive – but ended up being smashed in its shed by steam engineers who feared it would drive them out of business!

The first English patent for the use of rails as conductors of electric current was granted in 1840.

A Professor Farmer ran an electric car carrying two passengers at Dover, New Hampshire, in 1847.

In 1851, a road car built by Professor Page of the Smithsonian Institute reached 19mph near Washington – but the batteries were destroyed. Early battery-powered locomotives were clearly not viable, but the invention of the dynamo in the late 1850s and 1860s threw up new possibilities. It was discovered that a dynamo linked to an electric motor would cause its armature to revolve, and that armature could be connected to the wheels of a railway vehicle. Current would be supplied either from an overhead cable, or an extra rail laid alongside the track.

A small battery locomotive using a dynamo was tried in the USA in 1875, and at the Berlin Exhibition of 1879, a 3hp locomotive designed by Werner von Siemens hauled a train carrying 30 passengers along 600 yards of track, with a third rail laid between the track rails.

Siemens opened up a one-and-a-half-mile-long line at Lichterfelde, near Berlin, in 1881. It was the first public electric railway in the world. It ran at 30mph on 100 volts and the single locomotive could haul a train carrying 26 passengers.

The Siemens Electric Railway at the Berlin Exhibition of 1879.

Two years later, Britain's first public electric railway was opened, in Brighton – the Volks Electric Railway. The son of a German clockmaker, Magnus Volk was born at 35 (now 40) Western Road, Brighton on 19 October 1851. In 1879, he successfully demonstrated the first telephone link in Brighton. The next year, he connected the first residential fire alarm to the fire station. In 1880, he became the first resident of Brighton to fit electric lights (to his house at 38 Dyke Road), and over the next four years installed electric incandescent lighting to the Royal Pavilion and its grounds, the Dome, the town museum, art gallery and library.

On 4 August 1883, Volk unveiled a quarter-mile-long 2ft gauge electric railway running from a seashore site opposite the town's aquarium to the Chain Pier. Power was provided by a 2hp Otto gas engine driving a Siemens D5 50V DC generator. A small electric car was fitted with a 1½hp motor giving a top speed of 6mph. The following year, he widened the track to 2ft 8½in gauge, and built two more powerful passenger cars.

Magnus Volk – who opened Britain's first public electric railway.

Eventually the line was extended to one-and-a-quarter miles, but it was later cut back to the present mile, from Aquarium to Black Rock stations. Owned by Brighton Corporation, it is now the oldest surviving public electric railway in the world, and while some may at first glance see it as an anachronistic piece of public transport, it is nothing less than a national treasure of immense historic importance and should be treated as such.

For in a country where a huge proportion of the national rail network is electrified, and new routes like the High Speed 2 line from London to Birmingham are being planned, Magnus Volk, just like Stephenson, paved the way for so many more to follow…

Two cars pass at Halfway station on the Volk's Electric Railway, Brighton.

Volk's Electric Railway Cars 7 and 8 in sunshine, newly repainted in the 125th anniversary livery of maroon and cream.

Services on the Volk's Electric Railway's elevated sections often faced the brunt of storm surges. The shingle is now much higher, so the original viaducts are not needed.

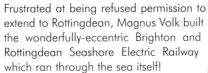

Frustrated at being refused permission to extend to Rottingdean, Magnus Volk built the wonderfully-eccentric Brighton and Rottingdean Seashore Electric Railway which ran through the sea itself!

It consisted of two parallel 2ft 8½in gauge tracks, billed as 18ft gauge, the measurement between the outermost rails. The tracks were laid on concrete sleepers mortised into the bedrock.

The single car used on the railway was a 45ft by 22ft pier-like building which stood on four 23ft-high legs and weighed 45 tons. It was powered by an electric motor.

Officially named *Pioneer*, many called it 'Daddy Long-Legs'.

It was equipped with lifeboats, and as well as a driver, a qualified sea captain had to be on board at all times.

Opened on 28 November 1896, it was hampered by storm damage and motors which were not powerful enough. It was closed in 1900 following beach erosion, and scrapped. Some of the concrete sleepers can still be seen at low tide.

The City & South London Railway which opened in 1890 was the world's first major electric line, the first electric tube railway and the forerunner of London Underground, the largest system of its kind. Locomotive No 13, built by Mather & Platt in 1913, is displayed at London's Transport Museum in Covent Garden.

Right: Preserved City & South London coach No 30, which dates from 1890.

Below: London Underground travel as it began: the interior of City & South London coach No 30.

The electric Liverpool Overhead Railway was opened in 1893. It could not use steam locomotives because it was too near to the docks. Pictured here in the 1920s, it was the world's first electrically-operated overhead railway, and also the first to be protected by electric automatic signals. Nicknamed the 'Dockers' Umbrella', the elevated line provided effective rapid transit for generations of Merseyside dock workers.

Below: A surviving Liverpool Overhead Railway car in the possession of the city's museum's service. The line closed in 1956.

It was also in 1893 that the 3ft gauge Douglas & Laxey Coast Electric Tramway using overhead 550V DC current opened on the Isle of Man. Four years later it was extended to Ramsey and in 1905 adopted its present title, the Manx Electric Railway. The line was nationalised by the Manx government in 1958. Tram 5, which dates from 1894, and a trailer are seen at Baldrine.

The 3ft 6in gauge Snaefell Mountain Railway running from Laxey to the 2,036ft summit of Snaefell, the highest point on the Isle of Man, opened in 1895, and still uses the same cars today. Overhead wires are electrified at 550V DC, with a Fell Incline Braking System installed between the rails.

The second tube line to open in London was also its shortest. The Waterloo & City line, which opened on 11 July 1898, runs for just one-and-a-half miles between only two stations, Waterloo and Bank, either side of the Thames. It takes just four minutes to travel from one end to another.

The next tube line to open was the Central London Railway, now the Central Line, in 1900. Six years later, the Great Northern, Piccadilly & Brompton Railway (the Piccadilly Line) opened, along with the Baker Street & Waterloo Railway (Bakerloo Line)... and as the underground network expanded, the capital never looked back. This 1912 poster extols the virtue of travelling beneath London by electric train, the underground network using a 630V DC fourth rail system.

A set of 1938 London Underground tube stock has been preserved in running order by London Transport Museum and is seen working a special from Amersham in September 2008.

The Metropolitan Railway was the world's first underground railway, but was first worked by steam. It was electrified in stages from 1905, when a new six-car train is viewed at Neasden Depot.

While only nine of its 34 stages were underground, the Metropolitan Railway eventually expanded to 80 miles, with electric trains facilitating the vast rise of west London suburbia between the wars.

Above: Seen running a special at Amersham in 2008, 1922-built Metropolitan Railway Bo-Bo No 12 *Sarah Siddons* is one of two survivors of its 20-strong class. The other, No 5 *John Hampden*, is a static exhibit in London Transport Museum at Covent Garden.

During 1909-22, the London & North Western Railway electrified most of its London inner-suburban network, using the same fourth rail system as the London Underground to which it linked. LNWR 1916-built suburban electric multiple unit (EMU) motor car No 28249 which is displayed at the National Railway Museum in York is the oldest EMU vehicle in Britain.

Siemens built this 750V DC shunter, D75S, for the London & South Western Railway. It was used on the third rail Waterloo & City underground line and is now part of the National Collection.

Left: The London & South Western Railway began electrifying its suburban routes out of Waterloo in 1913, choosing 660V DC third rail pick-up as opposed to the 6600V AC overhead supply of neighbour the London Brighton & South Coast Railway, which electrified its first line in 1909. A LSWR electric train is seen passing Cromer Road signalbox on the East Putney to Wimbledon line.

In 1926, the Southern Railway decreed that all of its electric lines should be third rail, because it was far it cheaper to install, with no catenary wires and support equipment needed, and so the inherited LBSCR overhead supply routes were converted. Southern Railway 4-SUB Motor Brake Third No S11179S, built in 1925 for work on south London suburban lines, is now in the National Railway Museum.

Right: This Southern Railway 2-BIL EMU set was built in 1937 to work long-distance semi-fast services on the newly electrified lines from London to Eastbourne, Portsmouth and Reading. The designation 2-BIL (British Railways Class 401) is short for '2-car Bi-Lavatory stock' as each set had two lavatories, one in each car. The Southern Railway third-rail network eventually covered most of southern and south-east England and there were 56 different designations of vehicles. This set, No 2090, is preserved at Locomotion: The National Railway Museum at Shildon.

Outside London, the North Eastern Railway began electrifying suburban lines in Tyneside in 1902, along with a three-quarters-of-a-mile mile, horseshoe-shaped Newcastle Quay freight branch line with gradients as steep as 1-in-27 and sharp curves. The NER looked to a steeplecab design of electric locomotive developed in the USA, and in 1904 two locomotives, designated Class ES1, were built.

Below: The two ES1s ran until 29 February 1964. One of them, NER No 1, is preserved in Locomotion: The National Railway Museum at Shildon, and is seen being inspected by Prime Minister Tony Blair when he opened the venue in October 2004.

Newcastle's Harton Coal Company pioneered the use of electric traction on its extensive industrial system taking coal and colliery waste to shipping staithes on the River Tyne. E4 is one of a near-identical pair of centre-cab Bo-Bo type locomotives built in 1909. It remained in service until the 1950s and on standby until 1982, when it was bought for Tyneside's Stephenson Railway Museum and converted to battery power so it can run.

Below: Siemens-Schukert four-wheeled steeplecab locomotive E2 was built in 1909 for the Harton Coal Company and is now preserved at Beamish Museum in County Durham.

THIS SIDE FOR | KINNING PARK
GOVAN CROSS | SHIELDS ROAD
COPLAND ROAD | WEST STREET
CESSNOCK | BRIDGE STREET

THIS SIDE FOR | ST GEORGES X
PARTICK CROSS | COWCADDENS
HILLHEAD | BUCHANAN ST
KELVINBRIDGE | ST ENOCH

SUBWAY

Nº 307

Nº

Left: The 6½-mile Glasgow Subway, which opened on 14 December 1896 as a cable-hauled line, is the third-oldest underground metro system in the world after London Underground and the Budapest Metro. It was converted to 600V DC third-rail operation in 1935. A replica station with vintage stock has been recreated in Glasgow's Museum of Transport.

Right: Unique North Staffordshire Railway four-wheeled wooden-bodied battery electric locomotive No 1 was built by Thomas Bolton for shunting the firm's copper works at Oakamoor, now on the Churnet Valley Railway, and famous for producing the world's first transatlantic telegraph cables. No 1 is preserved in the National Railway Museum at York.

Steam into electric: North Wales is world-famous for its narrow gauge steam railways built to serve the slate quarrying industry. However, in 1890 Llechwedd Quarry near Blaenau Ffestiniog converted its machinery to hydro-electric power. In 1927, of its Bagnall 0-4-0 saddle tank locomotives, *Margaret*, which had been supplied new in 1895, was converted from steam to overhead electric power. The chassis of another saddle tank, *Edith* of 1890, was similarly converted in 1930. *Eclipse* is seen operating in the 1970s. The quarry is now a major tourist attraction.

London's famous Post Office 2ft gauge underground railway between Paddington and Whitechapel once carried over four million items of post a day. The first section of the 6½-mile 440V DC centre rail pick-up line began carrying post in 1928, but running costs led to its closure on 31 May 2003. Several of the trains have been preserved: this one can be seen at the National Railway Museum in York.

The 'Brighton Belle' was the world's first electric all-Pullman service. Introduced by the Southern Railway on 29 June 1934, comprising three five-car EMU sets designated 5-BEL, it ran from London Victoria to Brighton until its controversial withdrawal on 30 April 1972. The 'Brighton Belle' is seen at London Victoria in 1961.

Below right: A 'Brighton Belle' set running through Merstham, as painted by G. Briwnant Jones. In 2009, a group under the banner of the 5-BEL Trust launched an ambitious £600,000 project to recreate a five-car 'Brighton Belle' set from five surviving vehicles for future main line use, filling a major gap in railway preservation.

Below left: Boarding the 'Brighton Belle' in its heyday.

The LNER planned to electrify its suburban line from Liverpool Street to Shenfield at 1500V DC using overhead pick-up, but the scheme was not completed until 1949, by British Railways Eastern Region, with electrification being extended to Chelmsford in 1956 and Norwich by 1986. Most of the London, Tilbury and Southend line was converted to 6.25kV overhead pick-up in 1962, and switched to 25kV two decades later.

In 1949, 92 three-car units (later Class 306) built to a LNER design were introduced. Withdrawn in the early 1980s, one unit, No 306017, has been preserved, repainted in a near original green livery.

Commonplace on the continent, the only double deck trains to run in Britain were Southern Railway Chief Mechanical Engineer Oliver Bulleid's two 4DD EMUs Nos 4001/2 for the Dartford commuter route. Despite complaints that the 'upstairs' was cramped, they ran from 1949 to 1971. Two driving motor cars survive.

The Great Central Railway and its successor the LNER both planned to electrify the 41½-mile Manchester-Sheffield 'Woodhead' route, and catenary gantries were installed before World War Two. The 1500V AC Manchester-Sheffield-Wath electrification project, including a new tunnel at Woodhead, was not completed until 1955. It ended up as the only main line in Britain electrified to this voltage.

Gorton locomotive works in Manchester provided locomotives for the route, EM1s (Class 76) for freight, and EM2s (class 77) for express passenger trains, Class 506 EMUs were provided for suburban services between Manchester, Glossop and Hadfield.

The prototype EM1, LNER No 6701 was built at Doncaster Works in 1941 to a design by Sir Nigel Gresley, and was later loaned to the Dutch government because the Woodhead project was not complete. One example, No 26020 – which was exhibited at the Festival of Britain in 1951, is preserved at the National Railway Museum.

Class 76 No 76046 in British Rail corporate blue livery at Guide Bridge on the Woodhead route.

The Woodhead route was controversially closed to passenger traffic on 5 January 1970 in favour of the alternative Hope Valley Line, and freight traffic ended on 17 July 1981, with most of the track subsequently lifted. The seven Class 77s were withdrawn in September 1968 and a year later sold to Dutch national railway operator Nederlandse Spoorwegen, where 1500V AC is standard. Following withdrawal, two were repatriated for preservation, E27000 *Electra* (pictured left) to the Midland Railway-Butterley, and E27001 *Ariadne* to Manchester Museum of Science and Industry. A third, E27003 *Diana*, is preserved in The Netherlands.

Below: Still in its Dutch livery, E27001 *Ariadne* stands inside its Manchester museum home.

British Rail's Doncaster workshops built 24 750V DC third-rail mixed-traffic electric locomotives in 1958 for the Kent Coast Main Line as part of the 1955 Modernisation Plan. Later designated Class 71, they hauled famous named trains like the 'Night Ferry' and the 'Golden Arrow' Pullman. In the late sixties, ten were converted to Class 74 electro diesels so they could operate away from the third rail system. All were withdrawn in 1977, and E5001 was preserved as part of the national collection.

The hallmark of the third-rail electric lines of the Southern Railway and its successor the Southern Region was the many varieties of EMU, which would need a volume of their own to cover fully. The 4-CORs (4-car Corridor units, BR Class 404) introduced in 1937 ran between Waterloo and Portsmouth Harbour. They were withdrawn from traffic in 1972. This example, No 11179 from set No 3131, survives in the National Railway Museum at York.

British Rail's 4-VEP Class 423 EMUs were built between 1967-74 and mainly ran South London outer suburban services in South London, and rural services in Kent and Sussex, before they were superseded in 2005. Two sets are preserved, including No 3417, restored by South West Trains to BR blue livery with painted aluminium window frames and sold to the Bluebell Railway for £1 for display at East Grinstead.

After slam-door stock was withdrawn from the national network in 2005, South West Trains obtained special dispensation to reduce two 4-CIG (Class 421) EMUs to 3-CIGS (removing one car) for use on the 6½-mile Lymington branch. One unit, No 1883, was named *Freshwater*, and painted in British Rail blue and grey livery, and the other, No 1888, was named *Farringford*, and returned to original Southern Region green, with the short route being rebranded the 'Heritage Line' Both were replaced by more modern stock in 2010.

Below: Glasgow's popular 'Blue Train' Class 303 EMUs were introduced in 1960 for the electrification of the North Clyde and the Cathcart Circle lines and ruled the roost on the city's suburban network for 25 years before being phased out and moved elsewhere. The last Class 303 operated on the North Clyde Line on 30 December 2002, Two cars are preserved on the Bo'ness & Kinneil Railway while very similar Class 311 vehicles are on display at Summerlee Heritage Park in Coatbridge.

The Southern Region's Class 73 Bo-Bo electro-diesels, of which 49 were built between 1962-67, are now unique in being able to run both off a 750V DC third-rail or from an onboard diesel engine, allowing them to operate on non-electrified routes albeit with less power. Several have been preserved while others remain in main line use today. Three examples are seen above at the Eastleigh Works open weekend in May 2009.

Following the publication of the British Railways Modernisation Plan of 1955, which called for the total replacement of steam by diesel and electric traction, the West Coast Main Line between London Euston and Glasgow Central was the first principal route to be electrified (in stages) at the new standard 25,000V AC overhead system. The first sections to be electrified were Crewe-Liverpool and Crewe-Manchester, and five builders were sought to provide 100 Bo-Bo locomotives.

Class AL1 E3003 (later British Rail Class 81 81002) is the oldest surviving British AC electric locomotive. It is owned by the AC Locomotive Group, which is based at Barrow Hill roundhouse near Chesterfield and has built up a magnificent heritage fleet.

The 25-strong class was built by Birmingham Railway Carriage & Wagon and were on passenger, freight and parcel trains. The last was withdrawn in 1991.

Ten Class AL2 (BR Class 82) were designed by Metropolitan Vickers and built by Beyer Peacock between 1960 and 1962 for the West Coast Main Line. The last was withdrawn in 1987. One is preserved, No 82008, and is pictured at its Barrow Hill home.

Fifteen Class AL3 locomotives were built by English Electric at Vulcan Foundry between 1960 and 1962. The last were taken out of service in 1988. One is preserved, in classic sixties electric blue livery, E30305, at Barrow Hill.

Ten Class AL4 locomotives were built in 1960 to a GEC design by the North British Locomotive Company in Springburn, Glasgow. The last was withdrawn from service in 1980. One example, E3054, is now part of the National Collection and preserved in its later BR Class 84 identity as No 84001 at Barrow Hill.

Forty Class AL5 (BR Class 85) locomotives were built by British Rail at Doncaster Works from 1961-64. Fifteen were later converted for freight use and redesignated Class 85/1. The last was withdrawn in 1991. One is preserved, E3081, in its latter-day identity of No 85101. Based at Barrow Hill, it was named *Doncaster Plant 150* 1853-2003 to commemorate the 150th anniversary of Doncaster Works, and is painted in Railfreight Distribution livery, which it never carried in service.

Left: A total of 100 Class 86 locomotives were built from 1965-66 by English Electric at Newton-le-Willows and British Rail at Doncaster. Following privatisation, examples were bought by several operators, with four being preserved by 2010, the first being No 86401 *Hertfordshire Railtours* (E3199), the only 86 to be painted in Network SouthEast livery, which it still carries. Also named *Northampton Town* at one stage, it is part of the AC Locomotive Group fleet.

Right: In a very rare if not unique example of an operational main line locomotive being named after a person who then buys it when it is withdrawn, Class 86 No 86259 *Les Ross* (E3137) is owned by Birmingham local radio presenter Les Ross. In 2008 it was returned to main line running order by Tyseley Locomotive Works in Birmingham and runs occasional special trains in its 1960s' electric blue livery.

Class 87 No 87035 is seen being raised at Crewe Works during the 'Great Gathering' open weekend in September 2005. Built between 1973-5 by British Rail Engineering Limited (BREL), the 36 class members were designed for West Coast Main Line passenger services. At privatisation, all but one were transferred to Virgin Trains, where they were withdrawn and sold off when the new Pendolino trains were introduced. The sole 87 still in use in Britain is No 87002, owned by the AC Locomotive Group.

In the sixties, British Railways axed all of the Isle of Wight railway network, traditionally a haven for ageing rolling stock from the mainland, apart from the 8½-mile Ryde Pier-Shanklin section which was retained and electrified. The electrification gave the opportunity to raise the height of the trackbed in Ryde's Esplanade Tunnel to reduce flooding at very high tides, but afterwards only trains with low clearances could be used. So for the 1967 season ex-London Underground electrical multiple units were brought in, firstly Standard tube stock built between 1923-31, which were redesignated Class 485, or 4-VEC (Vectis being the Roman name for Wight).

The Class 485s rusted in the Wight sea air, and were replaced by redundant Metro-Cammell 1938 tube stock, designated Class 483. In 2000, some of the remaining five 1938 units were repainted into a new livery of blue and yellow with pictures of dinosaurs on the sides – reflecting the geological riches of the island, and the nature of the ageing trains themselves!

Left: The 48-mile Tyne and Wear Metro, which uses a 1500V AC overhead supply and opened in 1980, has been hailed as Britain's first modern light rail system, combining aspects of elements of light rail, heavy underground city lines, and higher-speed suburban railway systems. The prototype Metrocar, No 4001, is pictured at South Hylton in 2005.

Right: Three Class 370 Advanced Passenger Train Prototype (APT-E) units powered by 25,000V overhead electrification ran in British Rail service between 1981-86, as a successor to the earlier experimental gas-turbine APT-E unit. Because of ongoing technical problems, the planned APT-S production series units were never built. This complete APT-E train is on static display at Crewe Heritage Centre.

Class 89 No 89001 Co-Co is the 1986-built prototype for a class that never went into production. The unique locomotive, built by British Rail Engineering Ltd at Crewe, was named *Avocet* by Prime Minister Margaret Thatcher on 16 January 1989 at Sandy, Bedfordshire, home of the Royal Society for the Protection of Birds, whose logo is an avocet. It hauled test trains on both the West Coast and East Coast main lines. Pictured in its former GNER livery, it was bought by the AC Locomotive Group in December 2006 and is preserved at Barrow Hill.

A fleet of 50 Class 90 Bo-Bo locomotives developed from the earlier 87s were built by British Rail Engineering Ltd at Crewe in the late 1980s, primarily aimed at replacing the classes 81-85 series. With a top speed of 110mph, they were fitted with a Time-Division Multiplexer to allow two or more locomotives to work in multiple, or to work a push-pull passenger train with a Driving Van Trailer or Propelling Control Vehicle.

In the early nineties, 26 were modified for freight traffic and redesignated as Class 90/1. Another five were dedicated to postal trains. In 2010, examples were being operated by DB Schenker, Freightliner, National Express East Anglia and Virgin Trains. Outshopped in InterCity Swallow livery, a Class 90 heads a North Berwick shuttle by Spittal on the East Coast Main Line in November 2004.

The 19-mile Docklands Light Railway is a light rail system opened on 31 August 1987 to serve the redeveloped Docklands area of East London. Extended several times, it has 40 stations over its 19 miles of lightweight third rail 750V DC track, much of it elevated with a speed limit of 50mph. Its trains comprise high-floor, bi-directional, single-articulated EMU cars – without driver's cabs because normal operations are automated. They are based on a German light rail design intended for use in systems with street running.

Below right: The 24 Class 442 Wessex Electric (5-WES) EMUs were built by British Rail Engineering Ltd and entered service in 1988 on the South Western Main Line from London Waterloo to Southampton Central, Bournemouth, Poole and Weymouth. The class holds the world speed record for a third rail electric train with 108 mph reached on 11 April 1988. No 442402 *County of Hampshire* is seen at Wool with a South West Trains service to Weymouth in April 2004.

The InterCity 225 is the fastest locomotive-hauled domestic train in Britain, and is made up of a Class 91 locomotive, nine Mark 4 coaches and a Driving Van Trailer. The 31 Class 91 Bo-Bo locomotives were built by BREL at Crewe and the coaches by GEC-Alstom in Birmingham, both as a spin-off from the Advanced Passenger Train project abandoned during the 1980s.

The 140mph Class 91s were ordered as part of the East Coast Main Line electrification project, which began with the King's Cross-Leeds section going live for trials in 1988 and the whole 393 miles to Edinburgh completed in late 1990.

The Class 91s entered service in March 1989. One of them, No 91010 (now 91110) holds the British locomotive speed record of 162mph set on September 17 1989, just south of Little Bytham on a test run down Stoke Bank. This example is heading south from Stoke Bank towards Greatford crossing near Stamford, carrying the livery of GNER, which lost its franchise for the route in 2007.

Class 465 'Networker' EMUs first entered service in 1991, mainly on suburban routes serving the south east of England, now operated by Southeastern.

Opposite: Class 373 EMUs provide Eurostar's high-speed rail service between Britain, France and Belgium via the Channel Tunnel. The first of 38 sets underwent tests in 1993. There are 31 'Three Capitals' sets consisting of two power cars and 18 carriages, including two with powered bogies and can carry 750 passengers. Eighteen of the sets, including seven shorter 'North of London' 14-carriage sets, were bought by British Rail and transferred to London and Continental Railways at privatisation.

A Eurostar set is seen in the award-winning St Pancras International station, alongside an example of Britain's latest electric rail sensation, the Class 395 Hitachi 'Javelin' train, on 6 November 2007, the day that the revamped former Midland Railway terminus was reopened.

The first of the Class 395s, the fastest operating domestic service trains in Britain, running at a maximum speed of 140 mph, was delivered from Japan to Southampton Docks on 23 August 2007. Operator Southeastern uses them for services from London to the Kent Coast. They can operate from either the High Speed 1 25,000V AC overhead supply or the local 750V DC third rail pick-up.

American poet and Beach Boys lyricist Steve Kalinich stands next to a Eurostar set at Brussels station on 14 November 2007, the first day of services from St Pancras International over the High Speed 1 rail link.

The Class 390 Pendolino EMU takes up where the Advanced Passenger Train left off. Fifty-three 9-car units were built between 2001-4 for Virgin Trains to run on the West Coast Main Line, using Fiat's tilting train pendolino technology. While it has a top speed of 140mph, track signalling systems restrict the units to a maximum 125 mph.

In September 2006, one example established a new speed record, completing the 401 miles from Glasgow to London in 3 hours, 55 minutes, beating the 4 hours 14 minute record for the southbound run previously set in 1981 by an APT-P, while the latter still holds the ultimate speed record for this route, taking just 3 hours 52 minutes for the northbound journey in 1984. The Pendolino fleet entered passenger service on 23 July 2002, at first from Euston to Manchester Piccadilly.

The Electrostar group of trains, which encompasses classes 357, 376, 375, 377 and 378, comprises the most numerous type of EMU introduced since British Rail was privatised. While most are third rail DC only, a coach in each set has a recess by which a pantograph could be fitted for overhead pick-up. The Class 375, built by Adtranz of Derby and which entered service in 2001, is the principal new train used by Southeastern, and can be seen on many routes from London to Kent.

A total of 67 Class 350 Desiro EMUs were built by Siemens AG between 2004-9, designed for use either on 25,000V overhead supply or 750V DC third rail. All 350s now operate in London Midland's livery. No 350108 is seen at Crewe.

While classic street trams are outside the scope of this book, from the eighties onwards the concept underwent a resurgence in Britain, with new light rail/metro systems taking shape in cities like Manchester (Metrolink, pictured), Sheffield (Supertram), the West Midlands (Midland Metro), Croydon (Tramlink), Nottingham (NET) and Edinburgh, in many cases using old railway trackbeds. One of the latest conversions involves a Metrolink extension to Rochdale taking over the Oldham Loop main line railway in Manchester. The wheel has turned full circle, with such street level lines echoing the pioneer Volks Electric Railway.

Credits

All photographs by the author or from author's collection apart from the following, to who grateful thanks are owed:

Volks Electric Railway Association: 9; Liverpool Museums: 12, 13; London Transport Museum: 17 (lower); Anthony Coulls, Locomotion: 23; Paul Jarman, Beamish Museum: 26, 27; Alasdair MacCallum: 28; 5BEL TRUST: 32, 33; Fred Kerr, 37, 43, 46, 55; Museum of Science & Industry, Manchester: 39; Scottish Railway Preservation Society: 43; Chris McKenna/Creative Commons: 50; Alan Lewis: 52; Transport for London: 56 (left); Phil Scott/GNU free documentation licence: 56 (right); London & Continental Railways: 59; Virgin Trains: 61; Greater Manchester Integrated Transport Authority: 63.

The Volks Electric Railway Assocation can be contacted via Membership Secretary Alan James, 13 Rudyard Road, Woodingdean, Brighton BN2 6UB, or at www.volkselectricrailway.co.uk

The 5BEL Trust can be contacted at 202 Lambeth Road, London, SE1 7JW, or at www.brightonbelle.com

For more details about the AC locomotive Group, which is based at Barrow Hill Engine Shed, Staveley, near Chesterfield, Derbyshire, please visit www.aclocogroup.co.uk